Widows
are
Warriors!

Widows
are
Warriors!

A Walk through the
Wilderness of Widowhood

Daily encouragement from a
Widow's Perspective

XULON PRESS ELITE

Xulon Press
2301 Lucien Way #415
Maitland, FL 32751
407.339.4217
www.xulonpress.com

Printed in the United States of America.

ISBN-13: 978-1-6305-0712-1

INTRODUCTION

Widowhood is a life-changing experience that can bring you to your knees, no matter whether your loss was sudden or anticipated. Each day brings with it its own challenges. Each day, you will ask questions about yourself and God. Each day, you will have to find the strength to move beyond your fears and tears. Each day, you will have to step into the unknown.

This, I know, you cannot do any of it in your own strength. However, you can do ALL things through Christ who strengthens you! (Philippians 4:13 NIV) This book is a compilation of my writings over a period of a year and half. As I walk this journey, I identify the various emotions and challenges that are innate to widowhood. Some of us struggle with understanding these emotions or how to deal with them; most of us think something is wrong with us because we feel the way we do. The truth is these emotions are common threads in the lives of a widow or widower.

Each day's reading tackles one of these emotions; I share from my perspective what it feels like to battle that particular emotion or experience. The narrative is real and visceral. It is not made to sound pretty or palatable; there is nothing pretty or palatable about widowhood! We are not here because we volunteered for the position. We are here because we were drafted into the position of widow or widower. Accepting this new identity is not easy. Yet, accept it we must.

How then do we come to terms with widowhood? How do we navigate through this journey? Where can we look for help? Deep within each of us is a strength we do not know we have because we have never been called upon to use it. Whether you are a person of faith or not, you will find the strength to take on challenges and navigate uncharted waters. My faith is what carried me through the troubled waters. I continue to cling to the promise of Scriptures.

I am confident that you will draw strength and encouragement from the words shared in this book; although written from a widow's perspective, the truth expressed applies to both widows and widowers.

INDEX

Day 1

WILL I LAUGH AGAIN?

Anhedonia is essentially a deficit in hedonic function; it is a decreased ability to experience pleasure, caused by a dysfunction in the reward center in your brain. It also includes a decreased motivation or desire for pleasure. When surrounded by what once brought you pleasure, anhedonia causes you to not experience that same, positive effect. Not being able to experience that pleasure also leaves you without a buffer from stress. [1]

While you may assume this is all about you being in a bad or sad mood, the reasoning behind it is really quite scientific. Dopamine is a neurotransmitter that goes off kilter when you are experiencing profound grief. This neurotransmitter is critical to the reward pathway in your brain. Without it, you cannot experience pleasure.[2] Your sadness, malaise, fatigue, and loss of appetite are not just something you can conquer by willing yourself to be happy. You cannot just wish this sadness away, nor can you fight it yourself.

Grief will consume you, and there is no denying it will reside in you for a long time. The decision to be made, however, is will you choose to reside in grief? Will you let it consume every aspect of your life? Or, will you choose each day to find a purpose for your life, and let that sense of purpose keep you moving forward? You may not feel like you have won, but as long as you are fighting, you have not lost either. So, put on your armor each day – fight by the power of the Spirit. This battle you wage is not against flesh and blood. Your enemy is not a person. Your greatest ally in this battle cannot be another person either. It is the legion of angels that fight on your behalf. It is the prayers of those who love you that will form a hedge of protection around you. While you cannot see or feel beyond your grief and pain, a battle is being waged on your behalf. You have to put on the armor of God – He will ensure no weapon formed against you shall prosper. Not even anhedonia shall prosper in your grieving heart and mind.

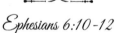

Ephesians 6:10-12
Finally, be strong in the Lord and in his mighty power. Put on the full armor of God, so that you can take your stand against the devil's schemes. For our struggle is not against flesh and blood, but against the rulers, against the authorities, against the powers of this dark world and against the spiritual forces of evil in the heavenly realms.

Day 2

BITTERNESS

BITTERNESS is defined as anger and disappointment at being treated unfairly; it is synonymous with resentment and envy.[3] As a widow, I feel all these emotions: ANGER at my husband for leaving me and cutting himself a good deal (Don't bother to tell a grieving person "he did not have a choice." I know. This is just a coping mechanism.); DISAPPOINTMENT that after twenty-nine years of working at a marriage, in the hope of growing old with the one I love, I am left without the ability to dream. It does seem UNFAIR in a world where people show little loyalty to their spouses and are constantly seeking greener pastures. Why my marriage? Why my husband? Why me? Why my children? I do RESENT not waking up next to my husband each morning, not drinking my morning cup of coffee with him, not receiving my daily three pm phone call, not having my gym buddy by my side, not having him sitting next to me in church, and the list goes on. I ENVY old couples — they get to reap the rewards after investing in their marriage over the years.

But, I cannot remain bitter. I have to remember that everyone, I repeat everyone, will have to endure the loss of a loved one. Death is inevitable. I hurt and I am in excruciating pain, but bitterness is hardly the balm that soothes my soul. GRATITUDE for what I was given, despite everything I have lost — now that is what I work at daily, not because it is easy but because it is necessary. It is a matter of survival. Bitterness will steal whatever semblance of joy I may have in my heart. Gratitude will allow me to live again.

Proverbs 14:10
Each heart knows its own bitterness,
and no one else can share its joy.

Day 3

CAN I DREAM AGAIN?

C an I dream again? It will have to be a decision — to dream alone is a foreign concept. Dreaming about the future, making plans, implementing those plans and fulfilling those dreams — in my life, that was always a "team sport." Twenty-eighteen (the year I lost my husband) was easily the most challenging and unforgettable year in my life; this year was all about surviving.

Twenty-nineteen was a year of change; this year was all about thriving. I learned a new skill: flying solo (figuratively); dreaming again; planning for the future again. Waiting upon the favor and grace of God that has so gently carried us through 2018, this favor and grace will continue to go before us and lead us to new pastures.

I pray that as you go through the first year of your loss, you will learn to rest under the shadow of the Almighty. Lean on Him. Let Him carry you. Your year of change and rejuvenation is right around the corner.

Isaiah 40:31
But those who hope in the Lord will renew their strength.
They will soar on wings like eagles;
they will run and not grow weary, they will walk and not
be faint.

Day 4

EMOTIONAL PAIN – WHAT'S IN YOUR FIRST-AID KIT?

These are the signs of emotional distress — sleep disturbances, dramatic fluctuations in weight/eating patterns, unexplained physical symptoms, temper control issues, obsessiveness, forgetfulness, chronic fatigue, memory problems, shunning social activity or any other pleasurable activity, and mood swings.

"The presence of anxiety, of a depressive mood or of a conflict within the mind, does not stamp any individual as having a psychological problem because, as a matter of fact, these qualities are indigenous to the species," says Charles Goodstein, MD, clinical professor of psychiatry at NYU Medical Center in New York City.[4]

Psychology Today lists five reasons why emotional pain is worse than physical pain[5]

1. Memories trigger emotional pain but not physical pain
2. We use physical pain as distraction from emotional pain, not vice versa
3. Physical pain garners far more empathy from others than emotional pain

4. Emotional pain echoes in ways physical pain does not
5. Emotional pain but not physical pain can damage our self-esteem and long-term mental health

Especially in dealing with grief, numbness can be a comfortable place – it is a whole lot better than feeling the full impact of your loss/pain. However, are you treating the cause or treating the symptoms? Yes, numbness serves a purpose, but it also postpones the full effect of emotional pain. Do you have something in your first-aid kit that helps you work through your grief and pain (thus working your way out of numbness)? Music, exercise, counseling, supplements and herbs to help reduce emotional stress, a grief program, or friendships that allow you to express your pain and grief rather than forcing you to "stuff" it – these would be essential items in your first-aid kit. If ignored, emotional pain can cause long-lasting and debilitating physical problems.

Matthew 11:28-29
"Come to me, all you who are weary and burdened, and I will give you rest. Take my yoke upon you and learn from me, for I am gentle and humble in heart, and you will find rest for your souls.

Day 5

GOOD GRIEF — WHAT ARE YOU DOING TO MY BRAIN?

Grief triggers a hormonal response in our bodies, which ultimately results in a very high level of cortisol, also known as the stress hormone. This persistent high level of cortisol can cause your body's immune system to be compromised, making you susceptible to infections and illness. The other stressors in your life do not help the situation at all. The flood of hormones disrupts the parts of your brain that are involved in regulating your emotions.[6]

What are some steps you can take to remedy this situation during this difficult time in your life?

- Take time out to eat well, exercise, and sleep. You will help your body and your mind recuperate from grief.
- Take some time off from work and daily responsibilities to process your grief. Instead of heading down a rabbit hole of negative self-talk – *Maybe I should have said something; Maybe I should have done something; Maybe it's my fault* – choose to delight in your happy memories.

- If you're struggling to think straight and get back to your daily activities, get help. Support groups can offer valuable resources to help manage grief.
- It's not uncommon for grief to evolve into maladaptive thinking. With some practice, you can learn to reframe nearly every situation to focus on the positive.[7]

Psalm 73:26
My flesh and my heart may fail,
but God is the strength of my heart
and my portion forever.

Day 6

HOW DO I SURVIVE THIS PAIN?

According to Dr. Earl Henslin, author of "<u>This is Your Brain on Joy</u>", *the emotions of joy and anxiety travel the same pathway in the brain.* [8]

In the midst of your unbearable pain, find a way to be thankful — not *for* what you are going through but *despite* what you are experiencing. Shift your focus away from your circumstances, where everything seems to be going wrong, and fix your eyes on all the things that are going right. Thank God for the people who stand by you and show up in your life when you need them, notwithstanding those you thought you could count on who repeatedly fail you.

Be thankful for what you still have — family, friends, a job, income, a home, health (you make your own list) — undeterred by everything you have lost (again, your list will be different from mine). Be THANKFUL in the midst of your pain — because that is how you will physiologically shove anxiety out (quite literally) and allow joy to rule your emotional pathways.

1 Thessalonians 5:16-18
*Rejoice always, pray continually,
give thanks in all circumstances;
for this is God's will for you in Christ Jesus.*

Day 7

LONELINESS

Loneliness — faithful friend of the widow. She has lost the one person in the whole world who she connected with at a cerebral, emotional, and physical level. Nothing and no one can fill that void. Long walks in crowded places are just as lonely as long walks on a deserted path. Dining with a group of fun-filled friends is oddly devoid of fun. Hearing others laugh reminds her of the sound of her own laughter, which once filled her home and her heart.

Psychologist John Cacioppo of the University of Chicago has been tracking the effects of loneliness. He suggests lonely individuals report higher levels of perceived stress, even when exposed to the same stressors as non-lonely people, and even when they are relaxing. The most profound statement he made is that the social interactions that lonely people have are not as positive as those of other people, hence the relationships they have do not buffer them from stress as relationships normally do. Loneliness, Cacioppo concludes, sets in motion a variety of "slowly unfolding pathophysiological processes." The net result is that the lonely experience higher levels of cumulative wear and tear.[9]

How do I battle this loneliness? Do I pretend I am not lonely; or, repeatedly put myself in places where I am surrounded by people who can't comprehend the depth of a widow's loneliness? Friends will honestly admit to not knowing what it may feel like. And, I admit that I did not know what it felt like until it became my portion. Like everything else — just because I cannot change it does not mean I should succumb to it. *"The Mind can make a heaven out of Hell or a Hell out of Heaven"* (John Milton 1667). As it eats at my soul, I fight back by trying to find that person I used to be; the person I know is still tucked away beneath all those layers of pain. I do whatever I can to ease my pain — maybe someday she will emerge. I hope I recognize her when she does.

Psalm 25:16
Turn to me and be gracious to me,
for I am lonely and afflicted.

Day 8

FORGIVENESS – WHAT ROLE DOES IT PLAY IN MY GRIEF JOURNEY?

Guilt and anger are recognized characteristics of the grief journey — Guilt over what could have been done or should have been done; guilt over things left unsaid or things that were better left unsaid; guilt over those fleeting moments where a smile might form around the corners of your mouth; guilt for some unknown reason. Anger over the circumstances surrounding your loss; anger about what your spouse should have done to take better care of himself/herself; anger over what you should have done to take better care of your spouse; anger about why any of this had to happen; anger about every secondary loss you suffer that overshadows the initial loss over a period of time.

How do we get past any of these emotions? The human spirit cannot survive, let alone thrive, under the constant onslaught of these negative and destructive emotions. Human nature requires a reconciliation of sorts to every conflict.

Forgiveness just might be the key to this resolution: forgiveness of oneself, forgiveness of one's spouse; forgiveness for things that were said; forgiveness for things that were left unsaid; forgiveness for hurts inflicted over the years of marriage; forgiveness for failures on both sides, as you traversed life together. In marriage, we have the opportunity to confront our own failings and that of our spouse. We have the opportunity to engage in discourse and dialogue, frustrate each other, laugh with each other, and cry with each other. Then, one day, all you are left with is your thoughts. Your head and heart are bursting with unresolved conflict; monologue arguments about why you have to go through this grief. However, nobody is listening; at least nobody you can be brutally open and honest with. Healthy dialogue with your spouse is not an option. Monologues, as frustrating as they are, come with a certain advantage. You control the narrative! You can make a conscious decision to forgive or be resentful.

Forgiving oneself and forgiving one's spouse every single time an unresolved conflict arises in your mind or heart is the only way to bring reconciliation. Over and over again, as often as doubt and self-talk begin to overpower you; you will have to make a conscious decision to confront your worst thoughts. You will have to make a resolution to forgive yourself and your spouse. Forgiveness does not mean conceding victory or denying wrongdoing, real or perceived. Forgiveness means breaking free of the hold anger and guilt have over you. Forgiveness grants you victory over your circumstances. Forgiveness frees you to love and be loved – love the life you had (even as you grieve the loss), love the memory of the person you loved through every challenge, love the promise of a future (whether single or with another).

Proverbs 17:9
*Whoever would foster love covers over an offense,
but whoever repeats the matter separates close friends*

Colossians 3:13
*Bear with each other and forgive one another if any of you
has a grievance against someone. Forgive as the Lord
forgave you.*

Day 9

FEAR OF THE UNKNOWN

A widow deals with uncertainty and insecurity in every arena of her life. When she loses her husband, she loses her friend and her sounding board. Every decision she makes brings with it the threat of failure – she has lost her safety net. Yet, life as she knew it is a thing of the past and she is compelled to make "new" decisions for this "new" life she finds herself living. Today has its challenges. Tomorrow has its uncertainties. Beyond that lies even more uncertainty and fear of the unknown.

Esther should have feared entering the presence of the king, but she did not; she knew she could die, but she was at a point of complete surrender to the will of God.

> Esther 4:16: "…. *I will go into the king, which is against the law, but if I perish, I perish.*"

I do believe, however, that it is not so much the fear of death but the fear of living with the unknown that has a hold on us. Let's look at Esther to borrow a source of courage. That is the kind of confidence we have to muster in our walk as widows: a confidence that comes from knowing that our future is unknown, but God is not. I may have lost my husband here on earth, but I can trust in the Lord to be by my side always.

Psalm 62:7
My salvation and my honor depend on God;
he is my mighty rock, my refuge.

Day 10

REMINISCING – DOES IT HURT, OR DOES IT HEAL?

How often have people tried to console you after the loss of your loved one with the cliché, "Thank God you have your memories"? My memories were my worst nightmare! They were constant reminders of my loss. They brought me no consolation. Yet, for others, they browse through pictures and videos reliving precious moments. Each of us has our own way of coping with grief. Is it healthy, however, for us to reminisce? Is there a certain period in this grief walk that is better for reminiscing? Yes and no.

I needed to learn how to function again. For the better part of a year and a half, I had my "fight" on. My memories made me weak, and I lost my resolve to survive. My loss was too painful; blocking out all those beautiful memories of life with my husband was just my coping skill. Yet, ever so often, a memory will pop back up – either on Facebook or in my mind. It will instantly send me into a tailspin. I will dwell on it for but a moment, take a deep breath, and tell myself to keep looking ahead. Surviving this nightmare has been my focus. No looking back; no looking around; no peripheral vision – single-minded focus requires tunnel vision. That is what has worked for me thus far. My grief in many ways is stuffed down somewhere in the deep recesses of my heart. Unbeknownst to me, it is eating away at the very essence of my person-hood. How do I strike a balance between grieving and not letting my grief get the better of me? How do I approach the future without losing the beauty of my past?

In some very unplanned and unforeseen ways, my past has revisited me. Today, on a short weekend trip, I made an impulsive decision to drive ten miles to the nearest beach. I had no idea where I was going except that it was the nearest beach. As I pulled into the parking area on this quiet Sunday morning, I saw before me landmarks that were so familiar. In an instant, I knew where I was – unwittingly, I had revisited the beach where my husband and I had our last weekend getaway just a couple of months before he unexpectedly passed away. Memories flooded my mind and sadness overwhelmed my heart; I found myself bordering on the state of panic. As I walked the beach, I relived memories, increasingly getting a sense of my husband walking by my side and missing his presence by me, simultaneously. Then grief took over. I sat on the bench we last sat on together – only this time I was alone. Pain seared through my heart. I wept like I had not wept in a long time. I did not want to leave because I felt like I was with him when I was there. I did not want to stay because I could not stand the hopelessness of the moment. Finally, the parking meter won! I drove away.

God has the incredible ability of orchestrating situations in our lives, in His time and in His way, to bring us back to a place of grief one more time. A place of grief and tears is also a place of healing. I am sorrowful yet thankful. I was ambushed by grief, but I believe it was just another necessary step in my healing.

Jeremiah 30:17
But I will restore you to health and heal your wounds,'
declares the LORD, 'because you are called an outcast,
Zion for whom no one cares.'

Day 11

OH, THE HEAVY WEIGHT OF THIS PROFOUND VOID IN MY HEART!

Sounds contradictory? It isn't. Ask anyone who has lost a spouse. That heaviness within us that we carry around through every sleeping and waking moment is caused by the profound void left by our dear, departed spouses. This is a paradox.

When a person has an organ removed, the body goes through changes, adjusting to this new, available space. Other organs around start to shift, the space could fill with fluids or connective tissue, and over a period of time, that once vacant space is occupied. Sometimes it is occupied by something new (like a transplanted organ); at other times, something pre-existing and familiar just encroaches upon that space. Either way, there is a period of adjustment. The human body tries to operate in the unfamiliar; over time, it adapts. Eventually, it develops into a different version of its former self. This version is not necessarily better or worse than the former, but it is different.

The loss of my spouse caused tremendous upheaval in my life. In so many ways, it is akin to losing an organ. Each morning felt strange — not waking up next to someone; not sharing a morning cup of java with someone; not having someone to make small conversation with; not having someone to share in major decisions; and, most of all, not having that quiet presence in your life that over the years feels like an extension of yourself. The two do become one in marriage. And when one of those two is taken away, it leaves you feeling like half a person.

The void I felt was painfully heavy; it consumed my sleeping and waking moments. I tried to run from it, but it went with me everywhere. I tried to crowd it out with busyness, but I felt stifled (like I was in a crowded elevator). I wanted to stop running because I was exhausted. I wanted to get out of that crowded elevator because I just wanted to breathe. Over time, I ran less. Breathing became easier. Eventually, I learned to live with my new self. I stopped feeling like half a person. I began to see myself as a "single" person, different from the one who was part of a team, a whole person who has learned to live life alone. There are days when I feel the absence of the other part of me. There are days when I embrace being "just me."

I still feel the void all the time — it just does not feel heavy anymore. It feels different. Strange in some ways but growing in familiarity.

John 1:16
Out of his fullness we have all received grace
in place of grace already given.

Day 12

THE LOOKING-GLASS SELF

The Looking-glass Self is a social psychological concept created by Charles Horton Cooley in 1902, stating that a person's self grows out of society's interpersonal interactions and the perceptions of others. You begin to see yourself through the lens of other people's opinions. Pretty soon, you think you are who they say you are.

There are three components of the looking-glass self, 1) we imagine how we appear to others, 2) we imagine the judgment of that appearance and 3) we develop our self (identity) through the judgments of others.[10]

I find myself applying Cooley's looking-glass self-concept to myself as a widow. People around me have opinions of how I grieve, how I navigate through challenges stemming from my husband's passing, and how I do life on a day-to-day basis. I hear these opinions and question myself. Sometimes, I chastise myself because I am grieving too deeply. At other times, I applaud myself for weathering several figurative storms in these last several months. Yet, I find myself taking to heart everything that is said and reading between the lines.

A widow's biggest challenge is "loss of identity." As she navigates through the mire of grief, she tries to determine who she is in this new life that has been thrust upon her. In that quest, she analyzes the validity of everything she is told. She may try to "fit the mold." Do I grieve too much or am I not grieving enough? Am I too strong or am I not strong enough? Do I plough through life as if nothing happened, or do I take the time to heal? Every decision she makes has social implications, because she is surrounded by people whose perception of her actions begins to shape her identity.

This is why a widow needs community, not isolation. She needs to be surrounded by widows who validate her as they navigate similar challenges. But, she also needs to be among non-widows, so she can develop her sense of self outside her new identity as a widow. She needs to be part of a conscious effort to integrate her into mainstream activities. There needs to be a concerted endeavor to move her from her innate response of self-isolation (fueled by a sense of abandonment) to a wholesome community of people who choose to understand and love her.

Romans 8:37
*No, in all these things we are more than conquerors
through him who loved us.*

Psalm 139:14
*I praise you because I am fearfully and wonderfully made;
your works are wonderful; I know that full well.*

Day 13

MILESTONES

Milestones are measures of your distance from a certain place or event. At first you measure them in hours, then days, weeks, months, and finally years. The first year — the most dreaded milestone that you want to put behind you is thought to be the most difficult year. Those who have not suffered a profound loss think it should be all roses and sunshine after the first year. Often, you will hear the comment, "Wow! It has been a year already? That went by fast." But the grieving spouse will tell you it was the longest, most painful year of his/her life; a year that was often navigated in two-hour segments because you lacked the ability to visualize the future or plan for longer periods. Your emotions were labile and, hence, your ability to make commitments or keep them were questionable. You counted down the days, not because you were looking forward to a certain milestone but because you told yourself it would get better with each passing day.

On the verge of "Year One," I was terrified. I hoped I would be stronger and more optimistic about the future. I hoped that by the time I reached this milestone, I would have the pieces of my life put back together again (even if they were just barely held together). I thought I would be able to look at photographs and watch videos and enjoy the happiness of the moments captured — but the pain in my heart seared through any joy I felt. In a sense, the pain is more real now; the numbness has worn off; the anger has dissipated; and reality is slowly sinking in — nothing has changed since that fateful day when everything changed. This loss is forever. Will "Year One" make something magical happen? Will it be that moment when you finally cross over from the desert into the promised land? Will it be less painful? Will it be a time of new beginnings, new dreams, new plans, and renewed hope for the future? I am afraid it may not be so. But I am hopeful that reaching this milestone will remind you that you made it through the worst year of your life–"Year One."

I will cling to the one who carried me through 'Year One.'

Isaiah 40:31
But those who hope in the LORD will renew their strength.
They will soar on wings like eagles;
they will run and not grow weary;
they will walk and not be faint.

I will entrust all worry about my future into the hands of He who orchestrates every aspect of my life.

Jeremiah 29:11
"For I know the plans I have for you," declares the LORD, "plans to prosper you and not to harm you, plans to give you hope and a future.

Day 14

MOVING FORWARD OR MOVING ON

Is there a difference? One just sounds like it has a negative connotation attached to it. Moving forward sounds like a step in the right direction, whereas "moving on" sounds like you are done with the past, you are done grieving, and you are ready to "forget." But, is there really a difference? Is forgetting an option?

Moving forward – "to advance forward while simultaneously causing someone or something to advance forward as well; to begin undertaking, developing, or making progress in some activity or project as planned." [11]

Moving on — "to stop focusing on someone or something in order to progress with other tasks or one's life; continue moving or progressing." [12]

Whichever term you choose to use — the outcome is the same. It all starts with a decision; a decision to not let your grief paralyze you. A decision to not let your past as a wife make you feel incapable of existence as a single person. A decision to not let your present status as a widow define you. A decision to not let your grief deny you the right to live and laugh again.

Once you have made that decision, you can choose to move forward or move on. You can embrace all that life has to offer you, despite the tragedy in your life. You can continue to find joy in all the little things, despite the pain of all the joy you have lost. You can find a strength you did not know you had and make decisions you never had to make alone.

Does this mean you are at risk of forgetting your beloved spouse? No, it does not! Forgetting is never an option, because the memories are ingrained in the very fiber of your being. It is a constant endeavor to "not remember." To block out the visions and memories of years gone by. To survive your loss, you do whatever it takes. Remember the good times and dwell on them or block them out because it hurts to remember. You get to do this the way you choose. It is your grief. It is your pain. It is your survival.

So, move forward or move on — whichever term you choose to use — just move. Don't remain static. Don't let sadness consume you. Don't let overwhelming grief be the hallmark feature of your widowhood. Move from "victim" to "victor." Your life has a purpose — fulfill it!

Isaiah 46:10
I make known the end from the beginning,
from ancient times, what is still to come.
I say, 'My purpose will stand,
and I will do all that I please.'

Day 15

SUDDEN LOSS VERSUS ANTICIPATED LOSS; DO WE GRIEVE DIFFERENTLY?

To begin with, every individual grieves differently; the dynamics of every relationship and our own unique personalities are always variables in how we grieve. To compound that, the nature of our loss also contributes another facet to our grief. Anticipated loss allows you to come to terms with the imminent passing of a loved one, but it also causes tremendous pain on a daily basis as you watch time tick away and a loved one slowly give up the fight to live. The grieving process starts as soon as you begin to lose hope of your loved one surviving. You have the opportunity to say everything you want to say, and you have the opportunity to forgive and ask forgiveness. You have the opportunity to shower your loved one with endless love. Yet, when you lose your loved one, the void is so intense because you have dedicated so many weeks, months, or even years to nurturing your loved one. Nothing else took priority in your life. And then, it is over. A very big part of your daily existence is now missing. You have lost your sense of purpose. You have to redefine yourself. You have to find new meaning in your life.

Sudden loss also left me with the same loss of purpose and loss of identity. The void is just as big and intense. The one, big difference is that I did not see this coming. I was blindsided. It hit me out of nowhere. Sudden loss is a different kind of trauma. It leaves your head spinning, and your thoughts are muddled. You feel like you were hit in the gut with a crowbar. The shock allows you to function through a daze. Reality sinks in and you realize you are only a shadow of yourself. Your processing is impaired. You fear for your own life and that of your living loved ones. After all, if it could happen once, what's to stop it from happening again? The final images of that traumatic moment haunt your waking hours. Sleep does not come easily and is punctuated with nightmares. Everything in your life is in disarray because there was no time to put things in order. It has been a year, and I am slowly finding the strength to fight back and live again. I will rediscover myself. I may even reinvent myself, because the old me is forever lost somewhere in the abyss. I will always wish I had the opportunity to say goodbye. There was so much left unsaid — even after twenty-nine years of being married. I would give anything to have been by his side in his final moments. After twenty-nine years of being married, I would have loved twenty-nine more seconds to say, "I love you, always." That aspect of my grief will stay with me forever. Sudden loss just leaves so many issues unresolved — there is no closure.

Yes, I do believe we grieve differently when our loss is sudden versus anticipated. We do not grieve less or more; we just grieve differently.

Joshua 1:9
Have I not commanded you? Be strong and courageous. Do not be afraid; do not be discouraged, for the LORD your God will be with you wherever you go.

DAY 16

THE PHANTOM SPOUSE —
MYTH OR REALITY?

I t has been said, "Losing a spouse is like losing a limb." Let's explore the validity of this statement. Drawing from my personal experience, the similarities are uncanny, to say the least. Both situations leave you without something or someone vital to your survival; that is unequivocal.

After an amputation, an amputee continues to feel pain/sensations in the missing limb; it appears this pain comes from the spinal cord and brain. During an MRI or PET scan, portions of the brain that had been neurologically connected to the nerves of the amputated limb show activity when the person feels phantom pain. After an amputation, areas of the spinal cord and brain lose input from the missing limb and adjust to this detachment in unpredictable ways. The result can trigger the body's most basic message that something is not right: pain. Studies also show that after an amputation, the brain may remap that part of the body's sensory circuitry to another part of the body. In other words, because the amputated area is no longer able to receive sensory information, the information is referred elsewhere — from a missing hand to a still-present cheek, for example.[13]

After losing my spouse, I continued to sense his presence. I expected him to walk into a room, to be sitting next to me, and sharing moments we would normally spend together. I expected him to show up when I needed help. I expected him to answer the phone when I called. I expected him to call me daily at three pm, as he had done for years. I expected him to be next to me on the treadmill at the gym. For a long time, my heart hurt while my head tried to process the idea that he was gone. Eventually, my head came to terms with that fact. I stopped expecting him to be there or seeing him in familiar places. My heart knew something was not right — that hurt. Trying to function with a gnawing awareness of a void in my life — that was painful. My heart is having difficulty coming to terms with what my head already knows: he is gone forever. The phantom spouse is real; slowly, his image fades. Someday, when my heart and head reconcile with each other, that image will be gone. I have to learn to walk again — using everything I have to compensate for what I have lost; knowing that each step will hurt like crazy, but acknowledging the only way out is through the pain. Reach for your "crutch" — whatever it may be and WALK AGAIN!

Isaiah 41:13

For I am the LORD your God who takes hold of your right hand and says to you, do not fear; I will help you.

Day 17

WAVES OF GRIEF

Waves of grief: they just never seem to end. They threaten to drown me. I cannot seem to come up for air. I flail in the storm. I panic. I cannot see ahead of me...and then I remember. Stay calm in the storm. When you are too paralyzed by fear to negotiate these waves, just roll on to your back and let the surge of the wave carry you with it. Oddly enough, this allows me to keep my eyes high above the storm, unto the heavens where my help comes from. Then I find that I CAN breathe. As my oxygen-deprived brain begins to focus, I realize I CAN tread water while I survey the ocean around me. I CAN anticipate the next wave, but better yet, I CAN see the shoreline. I now know in which direction to start swimming. My instincts to survive propel me forward, one stroke at a time. As many times as the waves threaten to engulf me, I will remember — roll, tread, and swim. As long as I am fighting, I am winning. It is exhausting. But I pray for renewed strength to do this again and again, for as long as it takes. Teach me, Lord, to wait — to soar, to run, and to swim. I cannot do this in my own strength.

Psalm 65:7
who stilled the roaring of the seas, the roaring of their waves,
and the turmoil of the nations.

Isaiah 40:31
but those who hope in the LORD will renew their strength.
They will soar on wings like eagles; they will run and not
grow weary; they will walk and not be faint.

Day 18

WHERE IS GOD?

I n the throes of my grief, I have asked this question. Oftentimes, I felt like He too had abandoned me. I took no consolation in the words, "God is by your side; He will carry you," because deep down inside, I knew He had the power to stop what happened. Yet, He did not. I questioned His agenda. Who is His next target? Me? My daughters? I feared He was out to "get" me.

Fear. Panic. Anxiety. Flashbacks. That is what the sudden loss of my husband did to me. I felt like the omnipotent God I had trusted all my life "did" this to me. I did not ask "why?" I knew the answer — "because He could!" He is all powerful.

As I worked my way through the mire and mess called grief, I was slowly able to remember who God had been to me for years. I realized He owed me nothing, yet He gave me twenty-nine years with my husband and much more. I repented of my sense of entitlement, as if for some reason I deserved better or more. I was able to see how He had carried me over the weeks and months when I could barely carry myself. I saw His continued hand in my life and that of my girls. I know for certain — He is the same yesterday, today, and forever.

Now, I see the vision He has for my life, a very different vision than what He had for me when my husband lived. I see that He still has a purpose for me — one that goes far beyond my own dreams for myself and my family. If you were to ask me, "Why?" My answer would still be, "Because He can. But most of all, because He has a plan."

Proverbs 16:3
Commit to the LORD whatever you do,
and he will establish your plans.

Jeremiah 29:11
For I know the plans I have for you," declares the
LORD, "plans to prosper you and not to harm you, plans to
give you hope and a future.

Day 19

ARE WE READY TO BE HEROES OF THE FAITH?

"We can be in our day what the heroes of faith were in their day–but remember at the time they didn't know they were heroes." A. W. Tozer [14]

As I grapple with a past that has been lost, a present that is so full of failures, weakness, and pain, I am crippled in my ability to see the future. Any future. Yet, it is my present and how I navigate it, despite my past, that will ultimately determine my future. Am I ready to be a hero of the future, even though I do not feel like one right now? Am I ready to just stay the course and do what I need to do today? I struggle with being able to dream about the future, but I have to trust that God has a plan for my future. I struggle with making it through each day, but I know His grace is sufficient. I struggle with the knowledge that I am so spent today and do not know how I will make it tomorrow, but His mercies are new each morning. Today – the here and now – that is all I am called to focus upon; to do what I am asked to do today;

to obey without assurance of outcomes; to step out in confidence, not in myself, but rather in the steadfast love of the Lord, which never ceases. The impact of what I do today will carry forward to the days ahead. As I do what I am called to do today, I am building a legacy, which will allow others in the future to see me as a hero of the faith; fearfully trusting each day.

Romans 8:18
I consider that our present sufferings are not worth comparing with the glory that will be revealed in us.

DAY 20

BROKEN-
HEART SYNDROME

Researchers have confirmed in recent years what people long suspected: extreme stress can literally break your heart. And as they learn more about the relatively rare condition, they are finding that it's not only caused by the loss of a loved one. Medical treatments, job loss, and other major life-stressors have been linked to this condition.

When a patient's heart "breaks," the main pumping chamber, the left ventricle, weakens, leading to pain and shortness of breath. The condition is reversible and temporary but can lead to complications similar to those after a heart attack. Experts think it's caused by a flood of hormones (such as adrenaline) produced during a stressful situation that stuns the heart.[15]

The loss of a spouse is an extremely stressful event; it triggers other stressful events, like a loss of job or productivity, loss of home, loss of confidence, loss of sleep, and loss of health. It results in an emotional upheaval, which leaves you without the ability to dream of a better tomorrow, constantly plagued by the sweet memories of what you have lost. You are consumed with sadness and loneliness. Your hurting heart is not merely an "emotional" phenomenon; it could be caused by a physical and medical condition. Be kind to yourself. Your heart is broken, at the very least in a figurative sense; however, if the condition persists, you should seek medical intervention. Find ways to control your stress and give your heart a chance to heal and recover.

Psalm 34:18
The LORD is close to the brokenhearted
and saves those who are crushed in spirit.

Day 21

CORTISOL: FRIEND OR FOE?

C ortisol is produced in the adrenal cortex in response to stress (physical or emotional) and according to natural cycles that tend to correlate to circadian rhythms. It helps us deal with stress by shutting down unnecessary functions, like reproduction and the immune system, in order to allow the body to direct all energies toward dealing with the stress at hand.[16] Therefore, what happens when your body endures prolonged stress, as in the case of grief? Let's take a look at the impact of cortisol on body systems.

Cortisol inhibits insulin from shuttling glucose into cells by decreasing the translocation of glucose transporters to the cell surface. All of this results in quite a bit of glucose floating around in the bloodstream. This puts you at risk for developing diabetes. Cortisol interferes with T-cell production and function, making your body more susceptible to invading pathogens. This makes you prone to infections. Cortisol inhibits the uptake of amino acids into the muscle cells, making it almost impossible to fuel muscle cells when cortisol levels are too high for too long. This weakens your muscles, making you prone to muscular injuries. Cortisol causes an increase in gastric acid production. When chronic, this can lead to reflux and other problems in the intestine. The decreased blood flow to the GI tract can also cause incredible problems with digestion. This makes you prone to GI problems. Cortisol and chronically elevated cortisol can cause intense hunger and food cravings, due to the metabolic derangement that occurs. This makes you prone to weight gain. Moreover, your adrenal glands get exhausted from constantly producing cortisol to keep up with chronic stress. This results in adrenal fatigue.[17]

As a widow, it is not uncommon for you to experience symptoms of fatigue, aches, stomach problems, and susceptibility to sickness. Knowing and understanding that these are not "in your head," but rather the effect of your immense grief and stress, may help you understand how to deal with them.

Philippians 4:7
And the peace of God, which transcends all understanding, will guard your hearts and your minds in Christ Jesus.

Day 22

DO WE EVER "LIVE" AGAIN? OR DO WE JUST EXIST?

L ife drags on. In one sense, it is mundane. In another, it is so full of unpredictability. Unexpected emotional peaks and troughs. Unexpected challenges to our emotional, psychological, and physical health. The inability to envision a future, to dream and plan, to have a sense of excitement. Each day is characterized by an overwhelming sense of despair. It's like watching a black-and-white movie — there are sounds, there is action, there may even be laughter: however, it lacks the vibrancy and luster of a movie in color. If all I had seen was black-and-white movies, it would not matter. My life was a movie in color, with emotion, laughter, sadness, joy, anger, frustration, and love. So, why is it black and white now? I guess when you take love out of it, the color scheme gets eschewed. Like a printer cartridge that runs out of a vibrant color, nothing prints the same anymore.

It is a real struggle to find joy again. You try to find happiness in the little things in life. Some days you succeed; other days you despair. On those dark days, you just wait and pray, because you know the sun will shine again. Each time you get thrown into the abyss; you remember that you were able to climb out. You were able to smile and laugh again. You give in to sadness, but then you realize you must fight again. So, you reach deep within yourself. You hope and pray you are not running on empty, but you know you've been running on reserve for a while. You heed the warning, "You are running low."

It is time to recharge. It is time to replenish. It is an exhausting process, over and over again. I do it because I must — I have two beautiful reasons to never give up: my daughters! That's all I need!

Find your reason. Everyday. Know your worth. There will be days when all you have is a sliver of hope. Cling to it. Never give up! Your life still has purpose, even when you cannot define that purpose. I cling to that promise.

———✦———

Jeremiah 29:11
For I know the plans I have for you," declares the LORD, "plans to prosper you and not to harm you, plans to give you hope and a future.

———✦———

Day 23

GOD IS OUR STRONGHOLD; A VERY PRESENT HELP IN TIME OF DISTRESS

As widows and widowers navigate the new and unfamiliar task of "doing life alone," may we be reminded that God is our stronghold and a very present help in time of distress. (Psalm 46:1)

Sometimes God rescues us from our struggles. He caused the shackles on Peter to fall off and the guards to fall asleep. Peter walked out of prison. (Acts 12:9)

Sometimes, He allows us to be thrown into the fire, but does not let it consume us. When Shadrach, Meshach, and Abednego were thrown into the furnace, the guards were burned from being too close to the furnace. But the three men in the furnace were not consumed...and they were not alone. King Nebuchadnezzar saw a fourth person in the furnace. (Daniel 3:24-25)

Sometimes, God will take what was meant to destroy us and use it to edify us. When Daniel was thrown into the lion's den, the rapaciously hungry and starving lion should have seen Daniel as nothing more than a meal. Instead, the lion behaved in an uncharacteristic manner. Because it did not attack Daniel, his persecutors recognized and respected the power of his God. (Daniel 3:28-29)

Psalm 91:14-15
"Because he loves me," says the LORD, "
I will rescue him; I will protect him,
for he acknowledges my name.
He will call on me, and I will answer him;
I will be with him in trouble,
I will deliver him and honor him.

Psalm 22:4
In you our ancestors put their trust;
they trusted, and you delivered them.

Daniel 3:24-25
Then King Nebuchadnezzar leaped to his feet in amaze-ment and asked his advisers, "Weren't there three men that we tied up and threw into the fire?"

They replied, "Certainly, Your Majesty."

²⁵ He said, "Look! I see four men walking around in the fire, unbound and unharmed, and the fourth looks like a son of the gods."

Day 24

WAS THE LOSS OF YOUR LOVED ONE LIKE A HURRICANE OR TORNADO IN YOUR LIFE?

W e were waiting and watching with bated breath. Hurricane Dorian progressively grew bigger and stronger in the ocean while the world watched. Those directly in her path knew she would hit – exactly when and how powerful she would be when she hit was anybody's guess. So, all we could do was prepare for the worst and continue to wait/watch. There was that fear the worst was yet to come.

As she swirled in the ocean, bands of strong wind broke off and drifted inland. For a few minutes, everything seemed to be chaotic, and then there was calm again. There was that small glimmer of hope that we may have dodged the bullet on this one. We continued to wait and watch. That is all we could do – prepare for the worst but hope for the best. Our expectations were lowered – we did not expect to be totally safe anymore. However, given what the worst-case scenario could have been, we were grateful for a slightly smaller challenge and a more manageable adversity. Little by little, our expectation of a normal life slowly faded, and we came to terms with the possibility of calamity. We told ourselves that we would be okay. We convinced ourselves that since the situation was out of our control, we would do the best we could and accept the consequences. Eventually, the hurricane passed by us. For some it brought total devastation, while for others it brought a lot of damage and destruction, but it was possible to piece our lives together again.

Recovery from a hurricane is long and painful; those living outside of the effects of this hurricane are quite clueless as to what it is like to wait and watch as your life slowly changes until the inevitable occurs. Some things are lost forever; some things remain as painful reminders of the waiting and watching. The helplessness, the futility of your prayers, the frustration of being totally out of options – this wears you out over a period. Then it happens, and a big part of you is relieved the waiting is over; the anticipation and hoping has come to an end. You look around you and take stock of your losses. You reach deep within you and resolve to rebuild and recover. Even though you were prepared for the worst, you were not prepared for just how much it could devastate you, your family, your home, everything that once held the fiber of your life. You are thankful for some of the pre-hurricane preparations you made. Yet, there were some things you did not think of or could not prepare for ahead of time. You just deal with those issues as they come. A hurricane devastated your life – you knew she was heading your way, but even the anticipation did not prepare you for the degree of devastation she would leave in her wake.

Tornadoes are a whole different story. You may not be aware that weather conditions are ripe for tornado formation. If you do spot one, you most certainly do not have time to do anything about it. You may get a few moments' notice, but there is nothing you can do to get out of harm's way. She comes at you packed with more power than you have ever seen before; she rips through your home, leaving behind a path of destruction like you have never seen before. In one brief instant, your life is forever changed. All you can do is struggle to get back on your feet and stare in disbelief. What was that? Where did it come from? Was I supposed to have anticipated it? Did I fail to see the signs? Did I fail to heed the warnings? Just questions without answers. Nagging thoughts of guilt and self-doubt. The devastation is so immense, you do not know if you can pick up and start again. You know you must, but you are paralyzed by the suddenness of the event. You find a way to start picking up again, but then you survey all you have lost; you lose hope of ever rebuilding and recovering. Those outside of the path of destruction cannot comprehend the magnitude of what just happened; everyone is shocked, but some think you need to move on. Almost everyone goes back to life as they know it, except you. You are left trying to make sense of what just happened. There was no preparing for this devastation. You first have to recover from the shock before you can begin to rebuild and put the pieces of your life together.

It may take you longer to recover from the damage caused by a tornado than that caused by a hurricane; not because the damage is any worse, but because you are in a worse state of mind to deal with it. Hurricane or tornado – your life is shattered, and you are not the same person you were before the storm. So, take care of you first. Once you are stronger, you can rebuild. Slowly but surely, you will be able to dream again and live again. But if you do not take care of you first, you will always find yourself struggling to think clearly and speak coherently. You will make wrong decisions and choices. You will compound your devastation. Take a step back after the storm has passed and survey the damage. Take stock of your losses, knowing fully well that some of them may never be recovered. Prioritize – ask yourself the question, "What do I absolutely need to take care of first?" Make a list of priorities and then work your way down that list. Make sure your health and emotional wellbeing are at the top of that list; if you don't, you will find it impossible to work your way down the rest of the list. Make sure dreaming again is somewhere in the middle of that list, because you should not lose all hope of dreaming.

Storms are inevitable – we do not live in the Garden of Eden. That was God's original plan; our lives on earth are "Plan B," for all of us have fallen short of the glory of God. Being mad at God for allowing the storm is pointless; questioning why some of us are struck while others get spared is a little selfish. Think about the time before the storm struck you; did you think you were spared prior storms because you were better than someone else? Likewise, do not assume that you are now struck as some form of punishment. Instead, ask God what He will have you do for the life that is ahead of you. We were not put here on earth to fulfil our own selfish ambitions; we are given breath each day that we may live out God's plan for our lives. Ask for and obey His leading. Your life has a purpose – live it!

Nahum 1:7
The LORD is good, a refuge in times of trouble.
He cares for those who trust in him,

Matthew 8:26-27
He replied, "You of little faith, why are you so afraid?"
Then he got up and rebuked the winds and the waves,
and it was completely calm.
The men were amazed and asked,
"What kind of man is this?
Even the winds and the waves obey him!"

Day 25

STAGES OF WOUND HEALING

Hemostasis: platelets adhere to each other, forming a thrombus which keeps the wound from bleeding further.

Inflammatory phase: fluid engorges the site, causing swelling and redness. This stimulates healing but is a very painful period. If this phase is prolonged, it can be problematic.

Proliferative phase: rebuilding of cells occurs, which leads to healing. The wound heals better if it is kept hydrated.

Maturation phase: the cells that were used for rebuilding are no longer needed. They die by apoptosis (programmed self-destruction) and are replaced by a more mature collagen.

This healing process starts about twenty-one days after injury and takes about a year. The new, mature tissue is only about eighty percent as strong as the original. There is usually a scar, something that will always remind you of the injury.[18]

As I apply the principles of wound healing to a grieving and broken heart, here is what I try to remember.

In the early stages of grief, shock works like a thrombus — it keeps you from feeling the full impact of your loss and pain, like hemostasis.

Then bit by bit, the numbness wears off and you begin to feel the full impact of your grief: this is painful and ugly, like the inflammatory phase. This phase serves its purpose to stimulate healing but staying in this phase for too long can be unhealthy.

Then you realize you <u>must</u> find ways to survive this grief; ways to take care of your emotional and physical health. You start investing in yourself as an act of survival more than an act of self-indulgence. It takes a while for you to realize you need to take care of yourself and for you to feel like you are going to make it, like the proliferative phase.

Finally, you realize there are some things that bring you joy and a renewed sense of purpose. You eliminate the things in your life that only helped you survive, and you focus on the things that will help you thrive, like the maturation phase.

If a physical wound takes twenty-one days to begin the healing process and a year to complete healing, do you not think a wounded and broken heart will take longer?

If a physical wound can be painful and leave permanent scars, do you not think your profound grief will devastate you and change you forever?

If you can learn to function and once again use a wounded limb, do you not think you can live again?

Be kind to yourself. Be patient with yourself. Healing is a prolonged, painful process. Someday, you will look back and see how far you have come. Until then, give yourself a hug for making it through each day. Heal well!

Isaiah 41:10
So do not fear, for I am with you;
do not be dismayed, for I am your God.
I will strengthen you and help you;
I will uphold you with my righteous right hand.

Day 26

"YEA, THOUGH I WALK THROUGH THE VALLEY OF THE SHADOW OF DEATH."

We all know that a mountain is the highest landform on the surface of the earth, and valleys are the low-lying regions between two mountains. Valleys are formed on either side of the mountain, and they are topographically contrasting. As the winds flow toward the mountain, they bring with them a lot of moisture and often harsh climate. As they pass over the mountain-top, they release all that moisture in the form of rain, which leaves the valley lush and green; a haven of sorts. A beautiful place to be. A place of abundance due to fertile soil, fed by the rivers flowing down the mountain side. This is the windward side of the mountain.

The other side is the leeward side of the mountain. A side "protected" from the harsh winds and rain; the result is a dry, arid ground that does not bear much fruit. This is the rain shadow area. However, one meteorological feature that is very common on the "lee side" of the mountain is – turbulence! As the wind crosses over the mountain ridge, it creates updrafts that could be two to twenty times the height of the mountain peaks! If you were thinking this was the safe side of the mountain, think again.[19]

This reminds me of the valley of the shadow of death – why is it we instinctively know this is not the lush, green side of the mountain, but rather the lee side? The windward side is full of life with its lush, green foliage and abundant fruit. That would be life as we knew it before losing our partners in life. Then came death. It hurled us across the mountain top and sent us tumbling down the lee-ward side. The valley of the shadow of death – an arid place of sadness; a place where joy does not rain upon us. We are promised that God is with us; His rod and staff will comfort us. But we can only stay here for a season. We were not designed to live in a state of prolonged sadness in an arid, parched environment. No – we were designed to be vibrant reminders of God's faithfulness. Yes, He will continue to be faithful as we claw our way up the leeward side of the mountain. We will miss our footing and slip several feet below, but we will recompose ourselves and start the fight back to the top once again. It will be a long arduous trek, but "His rod and staff" will comfort us. He will nudge us, guide us, and give us something to lean on when we are weary. Grief is exhausting! It is an uphill endeavor! But wait – what's on the other side of the mountain? You got it! That is what we were meant to do – live an abundant life full of purpose. As Ralph Waldo Emerson said, "The purpose of life is not to be happy. It is to be useful; it is to be honorable; it is to be compassionate; to have it make some difference that you have lived and lived well."[20] In that, may we find our happiness. I will see you on the windward side!

Psalm 23:4
Even though I walk through the darkest valley,
I will fear no evil, for you are with me;
your rod and your staff, they comfort me.

Day 27

TIPPING THE SCALES: TURNING OUR LOSSES INTO WINS!

Often quoted sayings leave me befuddled: Let go of your grief, wash your face, and get on with your life; lean into your grief; don't let your grief define or destroy you, etc. What do these mean to a grieving person? Does any of this help, or does it hurt? How do I respond?

Truth: nothing and everything is helpful. Nothing and everything is hurtful. It just depends on how I am feeling at the moment.

Some words motivate us to rise up and fight back against our grief, but on the days when we feel weak and defeated, they make us fight against the message itself. The very words that are uttered with the intent of challenging us to step out in strength make us recoil in frustration. We ask ourselves, is something wrong with me because "I am not there": is this even a realistic expectation? The answer is "yes and no".

We do feel defeated. We do feel like we will never get better. We look at other widows who seem to have it together. Then we meet widows who are so stuck in their grief they have lost any sense of purpose. We wonder — which one am I most like? We look for role models, and then we beat ourselves for not meeting expectations. We wonder if we will ever get there.

My experiences tell me there is nothing wrong with you, even when everything seems to be wrong with you. All the sadness, brokenness, hopelessness, and despair is normal. However, there is a danger in making that your new comfort zone. There is a danger in adopting that as your new identity.

Lean into your grief — let it take you on this painful journey. But don't adopt it as a way of life. Remember, there are twists and turns on this journey. WHILE YOU LEAN IN TO YOUR GRIEF, MAKE CERTAIN YOU ARE STILL MOVING FORWARD!

Wash your face and get on with life — yes, you will! But it will be in little steps. Make little decisions each day to be thankful for something in your life despite your pain. A negative attitude puts you on the losing team. You have already lost much — DO NOT LOSE THE HOPE FOR A FUTURE!

Get over your grief — one little battle at a time. Stop and think about your grief behaviors. You may choose to indulge in them because you feel so defeated; you choose the path of least resistance. But you must take little steps to resist those behaviors. DO NOT LET YOUR GRIEF DEFINE OR DESTROY YOU.

Certainly, easier said than done — like everything else on this grief journey. Surviving grief is a decision you must make with your head, despite the crippling pain in your heart. There is no getting over grief, but there is the business of getting on with life. The key is to find a balance and work every day to tip the scales in favor of you leading a productive life.

That is why I say WIDOWS ARE WARRIORS — it is not an easy task to fight these conflicting emotions on a daily, sometimes hourly, basis. But FIGHT we must and WIN we will!

Philippians 2:16
As you hold firmly to the word of life. And then I will be able to boast on the day of Christ that I did not run or labor in vain.

Day 28

WHY IS DEPRESSION COMMON IN WIDOWS?

Depression is the most common emotion associated with grief. As a widow, I feel no embarrassment in acknowledging this. However, understanding why you feel the way you feel is part of overcoming this hurdle.

When you are depressed, your self-esteem wanes and you may start to dislike yourself. "People with depression often think of themselves as "worthless, incapable of any achievement, and morally despicable." Why do people who are depressed have this negative self-appraisal? And what could be happening in their brains?

Choosing a self-descriptor means that you have to match the word with an impression that you already have of yourself. This matching process involves brain regions at the front and back of the brain. Like a well-coordinated rowing team, these different regions in the brain must be flexible and coordinated so that this matching can occur. In the case of self-appraisal, activation at the front of the brain (the medial prefrontal cortex) often moderates activation at the back of the brain (posterior cingulate cortex.)

As researchers had expected, when depressed patients reflected on themselves, the brain's front and back rowing teams were not coordinated. When the region at the back of the brain was activated by a self-descriptor, the front region overreacted when trying to control it. The greater the overreaction, the worse depressed people felt about themselves compared to control subjects."[21]

As a result, the brain had to work harder to establish some order too. (No wonder depressed people are often fatigued!) Although it was not entirely clear what specific aspect of depression was associated with this brain overreaction, the researchers found that it was highly likely that difficulty concentrating, and a sense of inner tension, were both affected in concert with these brain changes.

If you're depressed, know that the unstable connection between the front and back regions of your brain is making you dislike yourself and disturbing your emotional control. Your brain has lost its flexibility and accuracy.

That's why a relatively new treatment called self-system therapy (SST) has been shown to be so effective for depression. With this therapy, people who are depressed can achieve better control of their emotions. They learn to counteract their negative self-impressions. Unlike cognitive therapy, which focuses on reframing these negative ideas, SST doesn't focus on these negative ideas at all. Instead, it helps patients feel better by teaching them to focus on making good things happen by pursuing "promotion" goals that involve advancement, growth, and achievement. In fact, it is far more effective than cognitive therapy.

So, being aware that your brain distorts your self-impression is the first step in this therapy. Once you understand this, you can learn how to switch your attention to positive goals so that you can feel better about yourself again.

Job 29:24
When I smiled at them, they scarcely believed it;
the light of my face was precious to them.

Day 29

THE TALLEST TREE IN THE FOREST

Symbolically speaking, the tallest tree in the forest is thought to be the one which came from good seed, it was planted in good soil, and was surrounded by the perfect environment. This combination of factors allowed it to grow to its maximum and best potential, and be bigger and better than the trees around it.

Why then do I, as a widow, feel like the tallest tree in the forest? The seed I came from was far from perfect, the soil in which I was planted was quite tainted, and the environment that surrounded me was not free of contamination. I lived and learned as a young person under the cover of my father's household. He was the tallest tree in that forest. I grew up to be a woman and became a wife and mother; my husband was the tallest tree in my household. I survived and thrived despite the imperfections of my surroundings; I loved and was loved despite my faults and my failings. I enjoyed the benefit of NOT being the tallest tree in the forest. I enjoyed being able to hover beneath the branches of the tallest tree. I was sheltered from the storm. I was bruised but not battered, because the tallest tree would buffer me from the harshness of the storm. When I looked up, it brought me comfort to see the tallest tree looking down at me. When I was crestfallen, the tallest tree bowed its branches and lifted my chin. When the tallest tree felt the weight of the world on its shoulders, I leaned up against it and provided support.

Then the most violent of storms raged through the forest and ripped out the tallest tree from its very roots. As it came down, it damaged a lot of my branches. My foliage now bore a weathered and battered look. I keeled over, as my roots started to loosen from the soil. I was in imminent danger of being uprooted.

In fear, I looked up and realized there was no tree hovering over me; I had lost my cover. As I fought to keep from being uprooted, I found a way to steady myself. Every subsequent storm came with the threat of decimation. I had no one to lean on for respite. I knew very quickly that I was now unprotected from the elements and exposed to the harshness of the storms that swirled around me. As I looked down, I saw my children. I knew that I had to spread my branches around them and develop some core strength so they could be sheltered; I needed to be the tree they could lean on. I fought hard to be their shield; their source of strength and hope. When I stood as tall as I could to survey the damage around me, I realized I was the tallest tree standing. It was scary! I knew I had to find a source of strength greater than me, a shelter I could run to, and a source of calm in the storm. I looked above for help. There was no tree taller than me. There was just the vastness of the open sky and the brilliance of the sun. Beyond all of this was the Maker of heaven and earth.

Psalm 121:1-2
I lift up my eyes to the mountains—
where does my help come from?
My help comes from the LORD,
the Maker of heaven and earth.

Day 30

WHEN ADVERSITY STRIKES, HOW SHOULD I RESPOND?

I have dealt with adversity before – just not alone. Losing my husband as unexpectedly as I did sent me into a tailspin. I grasped at straws, trying to bring my crazy, spinning world to a stop or maybe even just slow it down a bit so I could regain some perspective.

I looked for help – there wasn't any to be found. My soft place to land, my husband, was taken away from me. The one person I knew I could count on to grab a hold of my hand and traverse treacherous waters was gone forever. I knew I had to do this. I knew this was how it was going to be for the rest of my life. I knew I needed to depend on something or someone that was everlasting and unchanging. I realized I cannot go through this level of despair and desperation again – not in this lifetime at least.

If there is one thing I know without a shadow of a doubt, it is that God is the same yesterday, today, and forever (Heb. 13:8). I will lean on Him. My years of knowing Him have taught me that He will never fail me. Even in my darkest hours, when I wondered if He had done a "bait and switch" on me, somewhere deep within was this hope that He was in fact the loving and caring God I knew Him to be. He is!

But then, who am I? My grief turned me into a person I did not recognize anymore. This was too much for me – what can I trust if I cannot even trust and understand myself? Once again, I had to turn to the Scriptures wherein I had for years found my identity. I asked myself repeatedly, "Who am I in Christ?" You see, my identity in Him will never change because He does not change. I had found my anchor once again.

God knows me because He formed me.
Jeremiah 1:5
"Before I formed you in the womb I knew you,
before you were born I set you apart;
I appointed you as a prophet to the nations."

I am chosen.
1 Peter 2:9
But you are a chosen people, a royal priesthood, a holy nation,
God's special possession, that you may declare the praises of
him who called you out of darkness into his wonderful light.

Day 31

THE WILL OF GOD

Do you feel like the loss of your spouse has left you feeling like a failure? The areas that you once considered your strength are now your failures. With the loss of your spouse comes a secondary loss of identity and purpose.

For a while after my husband passed away, I felt a sense of hopelessness and despair; I was convinced that God was on some kind of a demolition mission and I would be next. I frantically started putting affairs in order so my daughters would be able to do life without me and their dad. My focus was very short-term. I did not have to worry about the future because I was not expecting to have one.

After several weeks, I came to the realization that just maybe God was going to let me live – for what purpose I did not know. The only purpose I had in life was to carry my daughters through this horrific experience of losing their dad. Life was planned and lived in two-hour segments. There was no sense of purpose – I did not know who I was any more and I did not have the strength to figure this out. By default, I did the things I had done for years, but even in those areas I failed to excel. Soon I began to fear I would never be able to function again like I once did. This lack of purpose and mission made me question God's will for my life. I so wanted to live in accordance with His will and fulfill His purpose for my life but – what is His will for me?

Winston Churchill describes success as moving from failure to failure without any loss of enthusiasm.[22] Well, Mr. Churchill – I had the "failure to failure" part down really well, but the rest was a struggle. I learned to do the only thing I knew how to do: the next best thing. I did not know if it was good enough. I did not know if it made a difference to anyone around me. I felt like a ship without a rudder, just drifting this way and that.

How do I determine God's will for my life? I do not know that there is a clear-cut answer, except that bit by bit I find myself moving in certain directions and away from other pursuits. I do not know where the path I am on is leading, but I am going somewhere. A year and a half after being kicked in the gut, I am regaining my enthusiasm. Therefore, I believe I am heading toward success – from one failure to the next, fearfully trusting that God is directing my path the entire time. His will for me right now is to take the next step – no matter how tentative. I know I am living in the unfamiliar – I was thrown into that arena unprepared and without forewarning. That is the arena in which I learn to trust God more than ever. Less of me and more of Him!

Ephesians 6:5-6

Slaves, obey your earthly masters with respect and fear, and with sincerity of heart, just as you would obey Christ. Obey them not only to win their favor when their eye is on you, but as slaves of Christ, doing the will of God from your heart.

Day 32

DID GOD ALLOW THIS TO HAPPEN?

God's permissive will is what He allows to happen. The burning question in a grieving heart is, "Why did you let this happen?" Deep down, we are fully aware of the fact that God could have stopped it but chose not to do so. This makes us question His intentions and our own worth, as if God's purpose in creating us was to keep us happy and keep us content by giving us everything we want. We have it a little backward I would say!

God created us in His likeness and image so that we may do His will and fulfill His purpose for our lives. This sounds more like it is our job to keep Him happy and do everything He wants us to do. How do I know what His will for my life is? Will He speak to me in a dream? Will I hear an audible voice give me direction? Understand this, if God allowed something tragic to happen in your life, He intends to fulfill a purpose through that tragedy. You and I may not like it one bit, but He owes us nothing and we owe Him everything. Make a decision, despite your pain, to be thankful for the time you had together. Make a decision that your spouse's pain and death will fulfill the purpose God has for you, as you continue to carry the torch.

Romans 8:28
And we know that in all things
God works for the good of those who love him, who
have been called according to his purpose.

Day 33

WHAT DOES GOD WANT ME TO DO NOW?

Have you ever tried to figure out what God's will is for your life? I am most certain you have. I am also certain that you did not get very clear answers. So, how do we follow His will, especially after our lives have been turned upside down?

It is His DECRETIVE WILL – God's sovereign will – that determines the number of our days. We want to know why, but we get no answers. He can and does control everything. Therefore, we have no answers to so many questions – Why me? Why someone else? Why now? Why like this? Why didn't you stop it? Why didn't you make something good happen? Yes – He could have brought to pass everything you want Him to make happen, and He could have stopped everything that has brought you pain in your life. However, He did not. Yes – because He did not want to. This causes a lot of anger, may be even rage, in the hurting heart.

A loving God inflicting such pain on a person just does not make sense. He is "loving," but He is also "God." You and I do not get to call the shots and tell Him what to do. We may develop an attitude

and then say, "I have no use for God." Caution – we are just earthenware vessels among the vessels of the earth. Does the clay question the Potter?

Elizabeth Elliott says, "Today is mine. Tomorrow is none of my business. If I peer anxiously into the fog of the future, I will strain my spiritual eyes so that I will not see clearly what is needed of me now."[23] What is God calling you to do today? What does He want to do within you right now? He gets to shape us and mold us that we may serve as His vessels for as long as we live here on earth.

Are you ready to be "clay" in the hands of the Potter? Are you ready to let Him strip you of your own traits and make you more like Jesus? He is God. He will have His way. You can choose to willingly be part of His plan or painfully be coaxed into it. You will be a shining example of God's handiwork!

Isaiah 45:5-6
I am the LORD, and there is no other;
apart from me there is no God.
I will strengthen you,
though you have not acknowledged me,
so that from the rising of the sun
to the place of its setting
people may know there is none besides me.
I am the LORD, and there is no other.

Day 34

GRATITUDE AS A WEAPON AGAINST GRIEF AND ANXIETY!

On the verge of Thanksgiving, it would be apropos to discuss GRATITUDE as a means to counter GRIEF. These two antithetical sentiments are not innate to a widow or widower. Grief will overshadow gratitude repeatedly because it just consumes our hearts. Gratitude is a decision to consciously be aware of the positive in your life, notwithstanding all the negative and painful aspects. Moreover, a conscious effort to engage in "gratitude" despite your grief will cause your brain to sway the sadness of your heart. When we express gratitude, our brain releases dopamine and serotonin – neurotransmitters which affect your health, mood, and sleep cycle. They work as natural antidepressants. They have a direct effect on the area of our brain called the amygdala where our emotions, such as anger and fear, are born.[24]

As we take stock of our losses, it is so easy to lose sight of our victories. Robert Louis Stevenson once wrote, "Don't judge each day by the harvest you reap but by the seed you plant."[24] Take stock of what you have accomplished; every little mundane task is, in fact, a major accomplishment for a grieving heart. Every failure you encounter requires you to rise above it and overcome. Be grateful for these little victories!

Our brains emphatically do get affected by the trauma of losing a spouse. For weeks, months, and years, we are consumed with pain and sadness. However, we <u>can and must</u> choose thankfulness. We <u>can and must</u> choose to overcome. We <u>can and must</u> choose to live for a cause greater than ourselves.

This Thanksgiving, I am thankful for what I had in my twenty-nine-year marriage (even though it is a loss that hurts to the core). I am thankful for my ability to perform the daily tasks of life (even though I am merely a shadow of my former self). I am thankful for my daughters and the joy they bring me (even though it is painful watching them hurt for having lost their dad). There is much we have to be thankful for – all of us – despite all we have lost.

Have a Thanksgiving filled with GRATITUDE! May we overcome our sadness. May we overcome our grief. May we continue to honor our loved ones through the lives we continue to live – remembering them, loving them, and celebrating them through a life well-lived.

2 Samuel 22:50
Therefore, I will praise you, LORD, among the nations;
I will sing the praises of your name.

Day 35

PRAYER AND THE ART
OF SURRENDER

A grieving heart struggles with the concepts of prayer and surrender. I prayed that God would spare my husband's life, but He chose not to do so. So, what difference does my prayer make? What purpose does it serve? Does it actually change the mind of God? Well, if it does not change His mind, then why do I bother to pray? Does He even hear me? Does He care? The questions are endless, and the answers are not forthcoming. I stopped praying. I told God it was pointless asking Him for anything because He was going to do what He wants to do anyway. Yes – that is true. He will do what He wills, not what I will. When I pray, it does not cause Him to change His mind, but it does change my heart. Something within me begins to bend and conform to His will for my life. My prayer changes my heart. My changed heart changes my prayer. My prayer goes from supplication to surrender.

Surrender – that scary word which means I have no control at all. Surrender means no part of this decision is mine to make. Surrender means I do not "share" in the decision-making process; I merely get to follow where God leads me, wholeheartedly. Obeying grudgingly is not surrender – it is defeat; God won, and I lost. Prayer, however, has brought me to a place where I realize there are no losers on God's team. He leads us to victory when we realize the only battle that matters is the battle to do His will.

Jeremiah 10:23
LORD, I know that people's lives are not their own;
it is not for them to direct their steps.

Matthew 6:33
But seek first his kingdom and his righteousness, and all these
things will be given to you as well.

Day 36

WIDOWS ARE WARRIORS!
(Widowers are Warriors too!)

From wife to widow is not a beautiful meta-morphosis like caterpillar to butterfly — it is not a slow and gentle process; it is not something that happens within the privacy of a chrysalis, and it does not produce a fragile thing of beauty. As grief and pain chisel away at a once beautiful and confident woman who knew her identify as a wife, what she sees in the mirror each day is a patch-work of old and new — shades of her old self held together by pieces of a new and unfamiliar being. Most days she has to ask herself "Who am I?"-or as Mulan sings, "Who is this girl I see, staring right back at me?" This new identity as a widow is a painful pruning away of all that was once familiar — not just her weaknesses but also, in many ways, her strengths. It is a painful path to the emergence of a new woman — a Widow Warrior!

She once operated in a world where she expected to be validated and loved — she now has learned that she can (and must) rise above her expectations of herself in an act of survival.

She once felt incomplete without her spouse and soulmate walking alongside her on this journey of life. She now has to learn to walk as a widow — maybe with a limp, because a part of her has been ripped out of her very being. She finds her assistive device — anything that helps her move forward one painful step at a time because she can (and must) keep moving forward.

She once saw beauty in all she beheld and felt an overwhelming ability to give and receive love. She now smiles on the outside while her heart vacillates between numbness and pain, unable to give or receive love because that vessel of love, her heart, has been so shattered. Only time will tell how much it will be able to love and be loved, because she can (and must) love and be loved again.

She once felt she could conquer the world, because she knew she had someone to love her for better or worse. She knew she had someone who had her back. She had a sense of purpose because she loved that someone beyond measure, and each day she knew that somehow, they would help each other be their best versions of them-selves. She now drifts through the day afraid of failing, afraid of falling, and afraid that she does not make a difference in this world. She has to rise each time she falls, because she can (and must) — failure is not an option.

She will lose a few battles along the way — but the war itself, Oh! She will win the war! Because she can (and must). She will stumble through the darkness of that deep, bottomless pit of depression — but she will claw her way out. She will teeter on the edge of despair — but despite her stupor, she will hang on to some semblance of balance and keep herself from going over. She will be painfully aware of her sense of worthlessness and hopelessness, but she will rise again. Yes! Like a phoenix rising from the ashes!

She will be stronger than she ever knew she could be. She will be a force to contend with. She will traverse into arenas she would never have dared before, because now she knows she can (and must). She is a widow, but she is a warrior! Stronger than ever — watch out, world — she is a Widow Warrior! She will fight and win because He that is within her is greater than he that is in the world.

Isaiah 54:17
No weapon forged against you will prevail,
and you will refute every tongue that accuses you.
This is the heritage of the servants of the LORD,
and this is their vindication from me,"
declares the LORD.

Day 37

VALENTINE'S DAY FOR THE BROKEN-HEARTED

February 14th conjures up images of love and romance. Yet, some of us have only memories to hold onto. How do I celebrate this special day of love without the one I love? My heart, which still bursts with love, now feels heavy with pain akin to unrequited love. As much as I love my spouse, I will never hear him say those words, "I love you," which would so melt my heart. My memories bring me comfort and pain all at once. Therefore, that is not a place I can linger. The unfailing love of my husband had only been promised me "until death did us part"; all anticipation of eternal love can only be renewed when we meet in eternity. Hopelessness and sadness could be the hallmarks of this and every future Valentine's Day, unless I decide to not let it be so. In the midst of my loneliness, I choose to celebrate love — the love I once had, the love I continue to feel in my heart, the love I feel for those I still have in this world, and the only unfailing eternal love: the love of God. There will be sadness mingled with joy. But I am thankful that I once loved and was loved in a way that some can only dream of. Have a Happy Valentine's Day — even if it is not all you hoped for, even if it is not perfect, because what you once had and what you continue to have are worth celebrating.

Psalm 34:18
The LORD is close to the brokenhearted
and saves those who are crushed in spirit.

Psalm 147:3
He heals the brokenhearted and binds up their wounds.

Romans 8:3
For what the law was powerless to do because
it was weakened by the flesh,
God did by sending his own Son in the likeness of sinful flesh
to be a sin offering. And so he condemned sin in the flesh,

Day 38

ANTICIPATION – MY THOUGHTS ON CHRISTMAS EVE

The anticipation of an event, whether good or bad, typically lasts much longer than the event itself. The build-up to a moment of celebration is full of nail-biting excitement, eager anticipation, and hopefulness. The build-up to a fearful event is full of nail-biting stress, fear, and a sense of doom. As a widow, the two experiences of good and bad anticipation merge; what once was a pleasant anticipation now evokes a fear response. The events that once brought you much joy now are so full of pain, brought on by a reminder of sweet memories. Looking forward to annual celebratory events, like Christmas, birthdays, or wedding anniversaries, is now full of fearfulness and pain.

Memories of days gone by plague your thoughts and drive home your loss like nothing else could do. Christmas Eve — the night of anticipation of the birth of Jesus, the night of a reminder that there is hope for mankind — in our home was the night of music and singing around the piano. Now, Christmas Eve is the night of anticipation of increased sadness because of the absence of our "in-house Santa": my husband. Christmas would never be the same without him. Christmas has become to me a day I feared; I approach it with the attitude that it constituted just sixteen hours of wakefulness, which could be filled with busyness and distraction until I could go to bed. I eagerly anticipated the culmination of this once celebratory event so I could just go on with the business of day-to-day living.

It's Christmas Eve — for some of us, it is the first without a loved one...the first of many...the first of "forever without you." There is not much I can say or do to help myself or anyone else. While my heart aches and bleeds, while everything inside me is screaming — just the kind of screaming that is not comprehensible, yet so palpable within me — there is a calm voice that keeps reminding me to "Be still and know that I am God." (Psalm 46:10) So be still I will. There is not much I know anymore or understand except for this —

Romans 8:38-39

For I am convinced that neither death nor life, neither angels nor demons, neither the present nor the future, nor any powers, neither height nor depth, nor anything else in all creation, will be able to separate us from the love of God that is in Christ Jesus our Lord.

Day 39

WHY CHRISTMAS MEANS EVEN MORE TO ME AS A WIDOW

It's the most wonderful time of the year...and the most painful, nostalgic, nightmarish time of the year, now that my husband is gone. Our hearts and home scream for the void we feel. A voice that once boomed through our home at Christmas, as we gathered around the piano, is forever silent. The man of our house who wore a Santa hat and regaled us with antics straight out of the North Pole now rests in peace. At least, that is what celebrating Christmas feels like from our perspective. But is that all it is? Is there a reason to celebrate anymore? Are we looking at things from a lop-sided and grief- eschewed perspective?

The voice that once filled our homes with laughter now sings with a chorus of angels. The hands that played the piano to bring music into our world are raised high in praise of our God who never fails. The head that bobbed around the house wearing a Santa hat is now bowed in adoration of an omniscient God. Yes, Christmas is worth celebrating, because it is not about who we don't have with us. It is about who we hope to spend Christmas with forever. It is about who made Christmas happen — the Christ of Christmas. It is about the hope of eternity in His presence. It is about the promise of seeing our beloved again. Christmas without my husband means more than it did before, because while our hearts hurt and long for his presence here on earth — every time we think of him, we are reminded of who Christmas is all about. So, as we gather around the piano and sing this year, as we raise our hands in worship of the King of Kings, and as we bow our heads in adoration, we join in with our beloved who IS in the presence of the King. I hear his voice in my head and I see him worshipping with the saints. I hear trumpets and the piano fades away. He is celebrating Christmas every day with a passion and fervor we reserve for one day. What a glorious picture!

We wish you a Merry Christmas — we celebrate despite our pain and despite all the sadness in the world. We celebrate because Christmas is about Christ — the hope of the world. The only assurance we have of eternity in the presence of God. The only reason we look forward to seeing our beloved again. We celebrate Christ even more this Christmas and we look forward to the ultimate, glorious celebration in eternity.

Isaiah 9:6
For to us a child is born,
to us a son is given,
and the government will be on his shoulders.
And he will be called
Wonderful Counselor, Mighty God,
Everlasting Father, Prince of Peace.

Day 40

A NEW YEAR – THE PROMISE OF A NEW YOU!

The passage of time does not always bring with it an anticipation of a "new tomorrow." Somewhere deep within I know, "out with the old and in with the new" is an adage that is only partially true. Some parts of me have left me forever only in a physical and tangible sense; I still carry them with me every day and everywhere. Time may heal wounds, but the scars left from that gaping hole in your heart, those hurt. Tears bring healing, healing stops the bleeding, but the scars remain forever.

How then do we go on? Is it even possible to look ahead to a "new year" and a "new you"?

This year has taught me much, just as every other year does; these lessons, however, I would rather not have learned. I find myself drafted into the fastest-growing community in the world – the community of widows! Time has allowed me to come to terms with my new identity – it stopped the bleeding from my heart. Time also taught me that some things will always be a part of me – pain, sadness, tears, fears, and immense grief.

I was hoping that I will wake up one morning and just feel like my "old" self; instead, I have learned that I have to embrace my "new" self each day. My new self is not necessarily better than the old; but she works each day at being a better version of the person she was yesterday. Yes, it means working hard at not letting grief get the better of me. Grief may reside in me, but the new me must make a decision daily to not let myself reside in grief. We are unwilling partners in life – but we are not equal. Some days grief wins; on other days, the "new me" wins! It is these little victories I carry with me into the new year. The defeats of the old year have served their purpose – they have showed me resilience I did not know I had; they have strengthened my resolve to fight; and they have revealed to me the power of having a dream.

2020 – a new year, a new me (albeit with a lot of brokenness), a new dream that is ever evolving into something bigger and better than myself. That is the ultimate lesson I have learned, which I carry into the new year; I was created for a purpose bigger than myself. The "new" me will embrace that purpose, the "new" me will allow pain to fuel me, the "new" me will count not my losses but rather my victories.

The new me embraces my identity as a warrior, fighting a battle not of my choosing, but fighting, nevertheless.

Isaiah 40:31
But those who hope in the LORD
will renew their strength.
They will soar on wings like eagles;
they will run and not grow weary;
they will walk and not be faint.

CITATIONS FOR DEVOTIONAL

DAY 1: Will I Laugh Again?

1. Anhedonia, "Blood-Spinal Cord and Brain Barriers in Health and Disease," Science Direct, 2004, accessed January 09, 2019, https://www.sciencedirect.com/topics/neuroscience/anhedonia

2. Anhedonia, "Blood-Spinal Cord and Brain Barriers in Health and Disease," Science Direct, 2004, accessed January 09, 2019, https://www.sciencedirect.com/topics/neuroscience/anhedonia

Day 2: Bitterness

3. April 21, 2019,accessed December 22,2019, https://www.lexico.com/en/definition/bitterness

Day 4: Emotional Pain – What is Your First-Aid Kit?

4._Bouchez Colette, "10 Signs of an Ailing Mind," WebMD, 2006, accessed July 28, 2019, https://www.webmd.com/mental-health/features/10-signs-ailing-mind#1

5. Winch, Guy, Ph.D, "5 Ways Emotional Pain is Worse Than Physical Pain," Psychology Today, posted July 20, 2014, accessed July 28, 2019,https://www.psychologytoday.com/us/blog/the-squeaky-wheel/201407/5-ways-emotional-pain-is-worse-physical-pain

Day 5: Good Grief – What Are You Doing to My Brain?

6. Mayo Clinic Staff, "Chronic Stress Puts Your Health At Risk," Stress Management, Mayo Clinic, accessed November 18, 2018, https://www.mayoclinic.org/healthy-lifestyle/stress-management/in-depth/stress/art-20046037

7. Breazeale, Ron, Ph.D., "'Positive Reframing' as Optimistic Thinking," Psychology Today, September 25,2012, accessed November 18, 2018, https://www.psychologytoday.com/

us/blog/in-the-face-adversity/201209/
positive-reframing-optimistic-thinking

Day 6: How Do I Survive This Pain?

8. Persall, Kandy, "The Thought Train," Hungry
    for More Blog, 2018, accessed March 06, 2019,
    https://hungryformore.org/the-thought-train/

Day 7: Loneliness

9. Marano, Hara Estroff, "The Dangers of
    Loneliness," Psychology Today, July 1, 2003,
    accessed April 21, 2019, https://www.psy-
    chologytoday.com/us/articles/200307/
    the-dangers-loneliness

Day 12: The Looking-glass Self

10. Lesley University, "Perception is Reality: The
    Looking-Glass Self," Lesley University, accessed
    June 15, 2019, https://lesley.edu/article/
    perception-is-reality-the-looking-glass-self

Day 14: Moving Forward or Moving On

11. Farlex Dictionary of Idioms, Farlex, Inc., 2020, accessed January 25, 2020, https://idioms.the-freedictionary.com/

12. Farlex Dictionary of Idioms, Farlex, Inc., 2020, accessed January 25, 2020, https://idioms.the-freedictionary.com/

Day 16: The Phantom Spouse

13. Mayo Clinic, "Phantom Pain," Mayo Clinic, 2020, accessed January 25, 2020, https://www.mayoclinic.org/diseases-conditions/phantom-pain/symptoms-causes/syc-20376272

Day 19: Are We Ready to Be Heroes of the Faith?

14. Tozer, A.W., "Quotable Quote," Goodreads, 2020, accessed January 25, 2020, https://www.goodreads.com/quotes/349634-we-can-be-in-our-day-what-the-heroes-of

Day 20: Broken Heart Syndrome

15. Mayo Clinic, "Broken heart Syndrome," Mayo Clinic, 2020, accessed January 25, 2020, https://www.mayoclinic.org/diseases-conditions/broken-heart-syndrome/symptoms-causes/syc-20354617

Day 21: Cortisol – Fried or Foe?

16. Aronson, Dina, MS, RD, "Cortisol – Its Role in Stress, Inflammation, and Indications for Diet Therapy," Today's Dietician, Vol. 11, No. 11, P. 38, November 2009, accessed March 26, 2019, https://www.todaysdietitian.com/newarchives/111609p38.shtml

17. Jared Jagdeo, MD, MS; Peter R. Shumaker, MD, JAMA Dermatology Patient Page, "Traumatic Scarring", March 2017, accessed July 28,2019,https://jamanetwork.com/journals/jamadermatology/fullarticle/2604297

Day 25: Stages of Wound Healing

18. Maynard, John, "How Wounds Heal: The 4 Main Phases of Wound Healing," Wound Care Community, Shield Healthcare, December 18,

2015, accessed August 15, 2019, http://www.shieldhealthcare.com/community/popular/2015/12/18/how-wounds-heal-the-4-main-phases-of-wound-healing/

Day 26: Yea, Though I Walk Through the Valley

19. Weather NOAA, "Turbulence," Weather.gov, 2020, accessed January 25, 2020, https://www.weather.gov/source/zhu/ZHU_Training_Page/turbulence_stuff/turbulence/turbulence.htm

20. Emerson, Ralph Waldo, "Quotable Quotes," Goodreads, 2020, accessed January 25, 2020, https://www.goodreads.com/quotes/64541-the-purpose-of-life-is-not-to-be-happy-it

Day 28: Why is Depression Common in Widows?

21. Pillay, Srini, MD, "How to feel better about yourself if you are depressed," Harvard Health Publishing, Harvard Medical School, October 11, 2018, accessed September 25, 2019, https://www.health.harvard.edu/blog/how-to-feel-better-about-yourself-if-you-are-depressed-2018101115022

Day 31: The Will of God

22. Churchill, Winston, "Winston Churchill Quotes", Brainy Quote 2020, accessed January 25, 2020, https://www.brainyquote.com/quotes/winston_churchill_131188

Day 33: What Does God Want Me to Do Now?

23. Elliot, Elizabeth, "Quotable Quotes," Goodreads, 2020, accessed January 25, 2020, https://www.goodreads.com/quotes/1321824-today-is-mine-tomorrow-is-none-of-my-business-if

Day 34: Gratitude as a Weapon

24. Stevenson, Robert Louis, "Robert Louis Stevenson Quotes," Brainy Quotes 2020, accessed January 25, 2020, https://www.brainyquote.com/quotes/robert_louis_stevenson_101230